rainstorming Guide For Budding Investors

IONEY MANAGEMENT
FOR
INDIANS

I0510547

Partha P. Debnath

Second Edition 2024

PARTHA P. DEBNATH

Money Management for Indians

A Brainstorming Guide for Budding Investors

For my Parents
(Prabir & Tutu Rani Debnath)

Contents

Preface

Howdy Dear Readers! You have made a clear and hands down one of the best decisions to get this book. Now that you have decided to come along on this journey with me, I am humbled and proud that you have done it finally. This is the second edition (updated) of my first book on *Financial Literacy*. I have read myriad books on Money, Finance, and all those topics including Investing as well. But all are written from a foreign perspective and leaving a few, none of them has made a book for "Indians".

India is a developing country with people of sharp minds, great talent, and skills (which are taught or maybe inborn) but the money management skill is quite unaware of and most of us don't know the right way to manage our money.

In schools and colleges, we were neither imparted with any knowledge about money nor its management. We were just taught to work hard, get skills, and earn money. Never have we thought about how money management is essential and needed in the 21st century.

I believe that one of the most important skills to acquire is to know *'How to manage our money?'* than to know *'How to make money?'* You will receive ample advice from many pundits to get an answer for the latter but only a few will tell you How to manage your hard-earned money!

Throughout the book, I will address many time-tested formulas, and quotes from brilliant minds that will enlighten you in this process. You will gain a lot of insights (money wisdom) if you stick to the end of this book. I have spread invaluable **tips** throughout the book and you can start from any chapter you like. I won't say this will be the last book you have to read because Investing is a never-ending journey and learning has no endpoint. But yes, this book might prove to be a beginner's guide and will lead to the goal of attaining financial freedom.

How can you benefit from this book? Read actively, highlight the points that need your contemplation, take notes along the pages or in your journal, and finally after every chapter try to recall the concepts. This will ingrain the values in your mind. Make one of your buddies, a reading companion and share the concepts that you find intriguing.

Knowledge alone won't be helpful, so start practicing. With that, I hope you find this book an eye-opener on the concepts of managing money. If you are ready, shall we dive in?

1

Introduction

"He whose life has a why can bear almost anyhow."
- Friedrich Nietzsche.

There has been an ever-lasting debate about the role of money in our lives. Also, a few questions always strike our minds: Can money buy us happiness? Is money good or evil? We shall try to get an answer to all those questions. But before that, let's address a deeper question: Why?

This section is for those who want to ask me, "Why?" I mean why invest and manage money? Well living in a society where we have to fulfill our needs and wants plus if you have any dependents, follow up for them too. Someday, You will marry a good person, have children, increase your business, and have more luxuries.

Have you ever thought about how would you accumulate the capital to live a life of your choice? We are not always lucky to be born with a silver spoon. We might not have money left by our parents. Moreover, it is essential to know the value of money, which we can devise when we earn it ourselves.

Secondly, If you don't start early, you won't reap the benefits of Compounding (More on this later). Investing needs a little planning but more patience and time. No one is born with the knowledge of how to handle money. The sooner you learn, the better. You don't need to be an exception to be rich. You need to start!

According to the 2011 census, 74.04% of the total population is literate, but only a few understand the importance of financial literacy. As per the report conducted by the **Global Financial Literacy Excellence Center, only 24% of the Indian adult population is financially literate.** But why are these figures so crucial or even matter so much for us? Because unless we are financially literate, we can't make correct use of our money. The growth of the economy would be slow if you don't fathom the principles of money. A sound financial education and awareness is an asset for developing India.

Some of you might have a response: I don't have any money, I don't earn right now, I am in school or college. But as you move along the pages, you will come across various ways to invest your money even if you don't earn.

This book has been presented with the sole motive of **helping people learn the fundamentals of Investing and ways to manage money to lead a happy and sustainable life.**

Who can be benefited from this book?

- Budding Investors
- People who want better opportunities in life.
- People who are tired of being broke.

- People who want to attain financial freedom.
- And for all those people trapped in the 'Rate Race' and want to get out of it.

I assure you, if you start from today, follow each step meticulously, you can achieve wonders in life. This book is not a Get-rich-quick scheme. But it is a proven technique to attain a financially fit lifestyle. The book encompasses various principles and easy-to-follow methods that you can start practicing from day one.

2

Journey to Financial Freedom

"Working because you want to, not because you have to is financial freedom "
                                                              - Tony Robbins.

The financial needs vary from person to person. For you, it might mean something while for your neighbors or even your close friend, it might mean something completely different. Understanding this very first concept of Financial Freedom is indispensable.

According to definition, Financial Freedom is understood as being able to live the lifestyle of your choice while responsibly managing your finances. You could travel around the world without the guilt of spending your money.

It is the life you want to live without constantly thinking about Money (as a limitation). To be financially independent means to work only if you want to. Being financially free will also enable you to retire early and enjoy the rest of your life doing things that you crave the most.

For every individual, the goal is different. Some want an austere life with minimalism as their core ideology, while others desire lavishness and grandeur life. The greatest form of wealth is the ability to wake up every morning and say, "I can do whatever I want today". You can be financially independent with 1 lakh, 10 lakhs, or 1 crore rupees, depending on your choice. After deciding this amount, you need not worry about all the expenses. You can retire early too, giving time to your valuable ones.

You must understand that earning more money is not a solution to your problems. With an increase in income, it is normal that our expenses will grow too. It is important to know how to manage the growing expenses. The hardest part among the financial skills is getting the goalpost to stop moving. We have insatiable desires. The more we get, the more we want. To be financially fit, we need to address this issue too: When to stop? or What is 'Enough' for us?

Growing rich is 80% Behavior and only 20% Knowledge. What you would become tomorrow depends upon the tiny steps that you take today. Our habits decide our destiny. As James Clear ushered us, "Success is the product of daily habits, not once-in-a-lifetime transformations". So, start the journey taking those tiny 'financial' steps.

2.1 Setting your Goal.

In ideal cases, every new thing that you take in your hand should have a definite Goal. Without a goal, you can't achieve what you desire. Your goals should be **SMART**.

S for Specific: Be specific with your goal. Losing weight is a vague goal. Losing 5 kilos is a specific one.

M for Measurable: If you can't measure your goals, then you can't progress with your goal.

A for Attainable: Set an achievable goal. Losing 10 kilos in a week is not attainable. Ponder upon it and change accordingly.

R for Realistic: Make your goals realistic. Realistic in the sense that you can imagine yourself completing it.

T for Time-bound: Set a time bound for your goal. For example, I will lose weight (5 kilos) by August 31 of this year. This deadline is necessary to stay on track.

In money management, setting a SMART Goal is essential as well.

Before continuing with the book, set your goal. For example, I will save **25,000 Rs** by **25th November 2021** for **a new laptop**. Be specific, make it time-bound, and finally scribe your goal (maybe in a journal).

Based on duration, goals can be categorized into:

- **Short Term Goal(s)**: These are the goals that you want to fulfill shortly (anywhere between 0-3 years). Example: Getting new shoes, saving for travel, etc.
- **Middle Term Goal(s)**: These are the goals that you want to fulfill in the time frame of 3-5 years. Purchasing a new car or a new home might be a middle term goal.
- **Long Term Goal(s)**: These are goals set for a far future (5 years or later). Example: Saving for your retirement or your children's education.

Written goals have an enormous impact on our brains. Money can also be your goal. The easiest way to formulate an idea is to visualize it, feel that you have achieved it (as vividly as possible).

This principle has been highlighted in many books.

The journey towards financial freedom has been broken down into small pragmatic steps for your better understanding. Nothing can obstruct your way. The only thing that you should possess is a burning desire and perseverance. In the following chapters, we shall discover how money works and ways to manage it.

Let us first get the hang of how many types of income are there.

2.2 Types of Income

(a) <u>Active Income</u>: The income which we get when we work for it. We stop working, income stops. Sources of Active Income can be further divided into :

❖Income from **Employment/Job**s: You get paid by your Employer.

❖Income from **Self-Employment**: You own a shop and work in it. It is slightly different from the one above because now you don't work under anyone. Ex: Freelancing is a self-employment option. But, since it is also active, your income stops as soon as you stop working.

People who have a source of Active Income, have no freedom of theirs. They have to work continuously to get paid. You might be thinking what the other option is, right?

(b) <u>Passive Income</u>: Here comes the magical way of earning income without worrying about **doing work**. You have your freedom, time-schedule that is decided only by you. Here, you are the master. And since it is passive, you get money even if you stop working for a while (days, months, or even years). In passive income, money continues to flow for years and years.

Let's discover the two typical sources of Passive Income:

❖Income from **Business**: Businesses and start-ups are need of the hour if you want to have a passive income. Become a devoted businessman or an entrepreneur and bring some value to the lives of others with your product or service.

❖Income from **Investing**: Investing is the second pillar of passive income and is the core idea behind the book. It is a long-term method, so the short-term results are hazy. Dividends and Bonuses from companies are examples of Passive income.

Sources of Passive Income.

Passive income is the one that is profitable in the long run. If we work actively now to create a few sources of passive income, we can cherish the fruit of generating passive income in the future. You can generate many sources to get passive income. This list contains few options that you can go for. The List is non-exhaustive.

1. Invest in Stock Market and getting Dividend payouts.
2. Royalties for things that you created or contributed like books, music, etc.
3. Affiliate Marketing (selling other's products and getting a commission).
4. Create a course on special platforms and earn for every enrollment.
5. Create a youtube channel.
6. Sell your photography.
7. Build a podcast and create valuable content.
8. Rent out unused space.
9. Many more.

```
Tip: Passive income looks simple but you will start
accumulating riches only if you actively work for it.
```

2.3 The difference between Asset and Liability.

In his book called "Rich Dad, Poor Dad", Robert Kiyosaki had revealed the difference between an Asset and a Liability. According to him, an Asset is something that puts money in your pocket and liability is something that takes money out of your pocket.

Let's take "Our home" as an example. Many would keep it in the Asset section. But, according to the definition stated above, our home is a liability. Because it takes money out of our pocket in the form of maintenance costs. But if you keep that house on rent, It will be an asset for you (Putting money in your pocket).

An asset may also be illuminated as something that increases in value over some time in the future. For example, land of any category (Agricultural, Industrial, etc.) will increase in value and thus can be identified as an asset. On the other hand, liability is something that depreciates over time. A brand new car is a liability because the moment you go on for a ride, it loses its value by 30%.

To understand the preconception of money and to accumulate riches, it is indispensable to grasp the difference between assets and liabilities.

2.4 Why do the rich get richer, the poor get poorer?

The main reason why the rich get richer and the poor get poorer has been explained in several books. But here, I will try to simplify it.

- Rich people have a positive outlook on money. They don't vouch for the old idea that "Money is evil". According to them, money is not everything but just a means to lead a better life. The genuine rich mindset does not believe in showing-off. While most of the poor people have an outlook that, *Money is Evil* (that is the reason, they don't get it in the first place). I will highlight the simple statement: **Money, itself is No evil**. It just depends on who bears it and how he/she uses it. Wealth will make you more of what you are.

- Rich people know how to grow their money. They invest their money, increase their assets, reduce their liabilities. Rich people don't work for money, money works for them (Passive Income). While poor people have no idea how to grow their money, they have scanty knowledge of Finance. They don't invest or save, don't grow their assets, increase their liabilities. Poor people work day and night for money.

So, if you desire to be rich, study the habits and value systems of 'Real' rich guys.You should gather knowledge from the competent ones.

3

The Master Plan for Financial Freedom

"It is not about having lots of money. It's knowing how to manage it."
                                   - Anonymous.

You can't eat an elephant all at once. However, this massive task is not unattainable. It is a metaphor to explain that huge tasks seem unattainable at the beginning. But if we break them into small tasks, it can be achieved. As described in the book, Eat That Frog, "There is never enough time to do everything, but there is always enough time to do the most important thing."

As money management is a new concept for many, I have divided this into five steps. Each of the steps has been explained with ample details and examples.

- *Step 1: Become Debt-Free*
- *Step 2: Get an Emergency Fund*
- *Step 3: Initiate Savings/Investment*

- *Step 4: Get your Budget planning*
- *Step 5: Growing your Retirement corpus*

Step 1: Become Debt-free

The first step towards financial freedom is becoming Debt-free. Debt is the cruelest enemy in the path of Financial Freedom. You can't think of living a financially fit life without clearing all your debts. Debt is a vicious cycle. You should even resist giving debt to your close ones. Because once you give a loan you will set up a strained relationship (if the money is unpaid).

Dave Ramsey in his book "The Total Money Makeover" has formulated simple steps of reducing your debts and then becoming debt-free. You can follow the pathway by first, Paying the "minimum" of all your debts and then with the rest of the money pay the debt with the least amount, gradually paying it off and then going to the next higher debt. Becoming debt-free is an important step, as unfulfilling debts will cause you higher interest rates each month, creating chaos in your mind leading to stress and you would be far away from financial freedom. Remember that money is an excellent slave and a horrible master.

Tip: Try to avoid getting Credit cards. Even if they have a positive side(better credit score) but the downside is worse. Credit card companies (almost all) have hefty annual fees, hidden charges, etc. And once you forget to pay the credit bill amount, you will be charged a huge interest every month.

Step 2: Get an emergency fund

No one knows what ill luck may befall you and take away all your hard-earned money. Diseases, economic failures, job loss, and all other factors can reduce your savings. So thinking about these beforehand is better. Moreover, you can't predict the future. In general, it is advised to save for at least 6 months, so that you can manage during those months without having to worry about money. For example, if you earn Rs 20,000/month. Save 20,000*6= Rs 1,20,000 (for 6 months).

If you are not in favor of saving for an emergency, you can even think about getting *Insurance*.

Why must Insurance be taken?

Insurance is an agreement between the insurance company (Insurer) and the one who has opted for the insurance (Insured) that binds the Insurer to pay a sum of money to the Insured if something goes wrong. In return to that agreement, the insured pays a certain amount (monthly, quarterly or yearly) which is most commonly called the *Premium*. If something goes wrong, you (or your family) get a *cover*.

Opting for insurance is also a good option to save taxes. Under The Income Tax Act, 80C, you get a tax deduction of 1.5 lakh(Maximum). More on this later.

Before doing any investment, you should take Insurance as early as possible (25-35 years is recommended) because the older you get, your premium amount will increase as the chances of your death will increase with the years that you surpass.

How to select the best Insurance?

Never listen to a rogue agent who forces you to select an insurance that he tells you. Blindly choosing Insurance is one of the gravest mistakes you can make in your life. You must look for all the available options and then select the best for you. Some of the criteria that you can check for in an insurance company are discussed as follows.

(a) **Premium Amount:** Compare various companies online and choose the one with maximum benefits but with a lesser premium amount.

(b) **Claim Settlement Ratio**: It is the ratio of the number of claims settled by the *Total Claims*. Ideally, it should be above 90%.

(c) **Incurred Settlement Ratio:** It is the ratio of net/overall value of the claims by the total premium collected. This number should be 70-90.

(d) **Brand Value:** One of the biggest factors while selecting the insurance is to check the brand. You are buying the trust of a company. Choose a company which has been present in the market for a long time. Because you want your money in those grave situations.

Types of Insurance:

In India, several insurances can be availed. The most important are mentioned as under:

1. Life Insurance: Man is mortal. You can't ignore this facet of life. If you're the sole earner of your family (and have dependents), you must think about buying life insurance for yourself, so that after you die (I pray that you live long), your family can run. It is to be noted that life insurance should not be taken for someone who doesn't work.

Life insurance is again divided as Endowment Plans, Unit Linked Insurance Plan(ULIP), Whole Life Insurance, Term Insurance, etc. Here, we will get to know two main types-

- **Whole Life Insurance:** In whole life Insurance, you get a guaranteed cover for a time that will last for a policyholder's lifetime. In whole life insurance, you have to pay an extra premium and you get a set return. It is an insurance plus investment scheme.
- **Term Life Insurance:** Term insurance is for a specific amount of years (term). Suppose you are 25 years old right now and want to cover your life till 65 years. Then you have to take term insurance of 40 years. But you won't get the insurance amount if nothing happens to you in that term. You might think, I made the payment of all the premiums, and I don't get a single penny at a later stage then what is the benefit? In reality, term insurance is a better option than any other life insurance. Firstly, the premium amount are affordable, since term insurance is pure insurance (No investment involved and no returns promised) and the nominee will get the cover amount at the death of the insured. Secondly, a high sum is assured with very low premium amount.

How much cover should you take?

In ideal cases, take 20 times (recommended) your annual income. For example, if you earn 5 lakhs annually, then take a cover benefit of 1 Crore rupees.

```
Tip: Insurance providers also benefit from additional
benefits like the critical illness add-on, Disability
add-on, etc. These are called riders. It is better to
spend some more and add these riders to your policy
too.
```

2. Health Insurance: Your earning is fruitful and of use only if your health is stable and optimum. Accidents can happen anytime. You can't risk losing the money which you have saved. Just by taking health insurance for you(or your family), you can cover up all the medical and health expenses. These expenses will be paid under your policy by the insurance company.

While purchasing health insurance, look for a *cashless treatment* option in which the insurance company will handle all your medical bills (For the amount that you have taken cover for) directly with the hospital. Check the waiting period for Pre-existing illness, inquire about additional benefits like Ambulance service, availability of hospital room, pre and post-treatment expenses included, etc.

How much cover should be taken?

In general, take 2-3 lakhs if you are an individual, 5-10 lakhs for a family of four members (covered under one policy). Take an extra policy if you have elderly parents in your home. In

India, there are multiple schemes run by the government which provides free, cashless treatment for secondary and tertiary cases. These schemes may be helpful for taking care of the medical expenses and reduce out-of-pocket expenditure.

> Tip: You must disclose to the Insurance company, all the essential aspects of your lifestyle, any health issues you have, genetic disorders so that you get the insurance benefits or else your claim will be rejected.

3. Vehicle Insurance: Unlike any other insurance, motor or vehicle insurance is mandatory in India. In India, there are two types of vehicle insurance policies: Third-party Insurance and Comprehensive Insurance.

Third-party insurance is a mandatory requirement by law. It covers only damages to the third party. Under third-party insurance, you do not get compensation for the damages to your vehicle. A *comprehensive car insurance policy* covers both third-party liability and damage to your vehicle. So, before going for vehicle insurance, check for those features.

> Tip: Buy health insurance for all of your family members to manage the expenses in extreme situations. For Life insurance, buy it only for the person who is earning (and not for all). Do research the best companies before opting for an insurance. Also, don't mix Investing and Insurance.

Step 3: Initiate Savings and Investing

The best advice one can give you is "Start Investing". It is the golden advice and if you heed to it and perform your actions as mentioned in the book, then you are not far away from accumulating riches. It is important that you start investing as early as possible to reap the benefits of Compounding (The 8th wonder of the world). Just a quick reminder to you before you jump straight, investing is not a short-term formula or plan. You won't be a millionaire overnight. You have to pay its price. It takes something in return and i.e., Time.

Every investment has got some risk involved with it. Let us get a quick idea about the risks involved.

Types of risks

(a) Risk of losing capital: This risk can be handled by us. We can simply choose a safer option of investment to minimize this risk.

(b) Risk of volatility: This can't be controlled by us directly. Volatility is part of the stock market, mutual funds, etc. We have to stop continuously checking for the investment that we did, to avoid the upswings of our emotions. This will help us to think for the future as good returns are achieved only if we patiently wait.

So, if you can handle these risks and want to dedicate your time, we can start.

Types of Investors

(a) Retail Individual Investors (RII): These include Investors who trade in instruments (mainly Securities) for a value of not more than Rs 2,00,000.

(b) High Net-worth Individual (HNI): These include the retail investors who trade for instruments whose value is more than Rs 2,00,000.

(c) Domestic Institutional Investors (DII): These include Mutual Funds, Banks, Insurance Companies, Pension Funds, etc.

(d) Foreign Institutional Investors (FII): These are foreign institutions that take interest in Indian companies and invest in them.

Step 4: Get your Budget planning

John Maxwell has the best quote on budgeting, "A budget is people telling their money where to go instead of wondering where it went." But, you might argue that *Budgeting is so dull, it consumes time, I don't want to be restricted by a budget*, etc. Let me quickly state my ideology: **Budgeting is not a restriction on your spending but a clever idea of giving you extra freedom of spending the way you want**. Budgeting must be done to get your money managed the right way, plus spending the way you want.

There are various ways to start budgeting, two of which are introduced here.

The Envelope Method

In this method, the income you get is divided [keeping a set amount for Investing, usually 20%] into several different envelopes. These envelopes may be named: Rent, Food & Supplies, Bills, movies and eating out, etc. Each of these envelopes will get a set amount which you decide at the beginning of the month. Throughout the month you spend the money (from the envelope) for which you are spending. For example, if you want to pay the electricity bills, take out cash from the 'Bill' envelope. No cheating here.

If there is a shortage in one of the envelopes, you can use money from other envelopes. If required, you might increase the amount in one and decrease the other accordingly next month. This is a traditional way of budgeting. You can also use apps that are available online.

The basic principle involved here is to keep tracking the income and the expenses. It is not essential to be perfect and count for each and everything. But, we need to have a clear sense of how our money is being spent. There are no restrictions on spending. Do spend on things that you like, but cut the cost on things that you don't like.

The Kakeibo Method

Kakeibo is a Japanese term that means *Household Financial Ledger*. It is a physical (journal) method for budgeting. In this method, first, you deduct fixed expenses from your income; the rest of that amount will be used for various purposes. You need to keep a notebook and put your spending or expenses into **four categories:**

- **Needs:** Things without which you can't live (Food, House, etc.)
- **Wants:** Things which are important but without which you can survive (Shoes, eating out, etc.)
- **Culture:** Things like books, museum visits, etc.
- **Unexpected**: Things you weren't anticipating, like a doctor's visit or car repair

Kakeibo is different from other methods in the way that you need to write. Writing switches your thinking cap 'on'. You get a clear idea about the spending you do in the month. Thus, it is a reflective method.

50/30/20 Principle

The most ideal way to divide your budgeting is by this rule.

- Get your monthly income.
- Half of it (50%) will be used for spending on your Needs.
- 30% to your Wants (Travel, Movies, Eating out, etc.)
- 20% to the investments.

These are just a few methods to get an understanding of how to start Investing. You can tweak it according to your lifestyle and goals. For example, you can increase the 20% of your income for the investment to 30%, reducing the wants appropriately.

Remember that investing should be done vigorously in the early twenties or thirties so that compounding can happen. But also don't forget to 'bless' yourself with some perks and luxuries in the life that you are living right now.

```
Tip: Spending in cash is a better option as you will
not be a victim of "Impulse Buying". It helps you to
keep track of how much you have spent, telling you
when to stop.
```

Step 5: Growing your Retirement corpus

Start saving for retirement as soon as you start earning money and you have a backup scheme known as the "Emergency Fund" beforehand. You must invest now (for your retirement) if you want to spend your golden days in dignity. When you can comfortably live on your investment/saving income, you are financially secure. Retirement does not mean you stop working. It simply means that you don't have to depend on money for your living expenses. After you have saved the retirement corpus, you can start to live your life. May be you always wanted to write a book or travel around the world; now you can do it all.

Some of the popular *Retirement/Pension schemes* available in India are:

1. **Employee Provident Fund (EPF):** It is a 401k of India. You contribute it along with your Company/Employer. The employer and the employee each contribute 12% of the employee's basic salary (including Dearness Allowance). The money gets an annual rate of interest that is paid as pension when you retire. Currently, the rate of interest on EPF deposits is 8.1% p.a (approx). After getting

yourself subscribed under this scheme, you will be given a UAN (Universal Account Number). EPF comes under the tax category of Exempt-Exempt-Exempt (with some exceptions).

2. **National Pension System (NPS)**: NPS is a good option to get your money invested in the right hands. Under NPS, employees contribute 10% while the government 14%. In NPS, we can accept stock market returns because a part of the money we contribute in NPS gets invested in the Stocks. How much will be invested in stocks depends on us. We can choose it by our risk appetite or else leave it automated (with your age and risk profile). The minimum amount "per contribution" is 500. At the age of 60 years, you can withdraw a partial amount, while the rest needs to be used for purchasing Annuity (Pensions). There are tax benefits in NPS (More on tax saving later). You will get a Permanent Retirement Account Number (PRAN) which is a 12 digit number that identifies individuals who have registered under the National Pension Scheme.

3. **Public Provident Fund (PPF)**: It is considered one of the safest options. Unlike NPS, PPF is for a 15 years duration (called the Lock-in period), which can be extended in a block of 5 years. PPF is not linked to the market, that's the reason it is safer. While writing, the Interest rate of PPF is 7.1%. The minimum yearly contribution is Rs 500. PPF falls in the tax category, EEE (Exempt-Exempt-Exempt).

4. **Atal Pension Yojana(APY)**: APY is another beneficial scheme to get your money saved for your retirement. The goal of the scheme is to ensure that no Indian citizen has to worry about any illness, accidents, or diseases in old age, giving a sense of security. To avail this scheme, you

need to be between the age bracket of 18-40 years. You should contribute for at least 20 years. You can withdraw the corpus on attaining 60 years in the form of a pension.

5. **Unified Pension Scheme (UPS):** It is a new scheme which was introduced in recent times as an alternative to NPS. The government's contribution is set at 18.5% with the employee's contribution at 10%. The UPS offers guaranteed pension of 50% of the average pay for the last 12 months for the ones who have been employed for 25 years or more. Employees with at least 10 years of service are entitled to receive a minimum pension of Rs 10,000 per month. Both the assured pension and family pension (in case of employee's death) are subject to adjustment due to Inflation.

4

Start investing even if you don't earn

"If you don't find a way to make money while you sleep, you will work until you die."
- Warren Buffett.

You might say, "Partha, I think you've lost your consciousness". I would respond to that with a simple example about myself. In my family, my mom and dad are not well versed in financial knowledge. We are a middle-class family. There is no shortage of money, we live a decent life. But I can get a better life with more money (I am not greedy here, it's just a wish about how we can manage money, the right way to get more benefits and luxuries that can make our lives better).

So, at the age of 18-19 years, I started discovering all the knowledge regarding the ideologies that I have shared with you throughout this book. I would say this wasn't easy. But I did it. I read books on money, finance, investments, went through tons of videos online, talked with my buddies (got their ideas too).

After all this, I started sharing my newly discovered ideas with my parents. They were fascinated. I told them about all those investing methods, we can apply. There are chances to grow our money if we cleverly put it in the right instruments. Moreover, it is safer to invest in Mutual funds, stocks, or other investment options than to just gamble around (which has more risk of losing our money).

In this way, I convinced my parents to start investing. Yes, it was not my money of course, but seeing my dedication and goodwill, they took a chance starting with a small amount of money, and they didn't regret it.

To start early is what I would recommend to you. In this journey of financial freedom, you might have to say **No** to many things. Say a straight No to anything that doesn't increase your worth or value. For you to do something new and great, you must stop doing something old and ordinary.

To start a fresh venture, you will always have a self-doubt about: Is it the best time or not? This had come to me as well. I simply got over this by "Starting". There never comes a perfect time for you to start something anew. The universe *won't* align all the stars for you to give a kick start support.

You have to overcome being lazy, start saving, take advice from competent ones, and of course follow this book.

Tip: The best time to start investing was 10 years ago and the next best time is today.

5

Investment Instruments in India

"Don't wait for better investment options, invest and then wait for better time."
- Ankit Samrat.

Like any other country, there are several investment instruments in India. Some of them are extremely popular while others are quite obscure. But I have tried to include almost all of them.

5.1 Savings Account

The very first option we have and hear from everyone is to save our money in Banks and Financial Institutions. This advice is quite obsolete in the 21st century. Let me explain to you why. We save in a bank that provides us a 4-5 % interest rate annually. We feel content with it. But very few people think about the Inflation rate that eats up our returns every year. The average inflation rate per year for the past 63 years was 7.5% So, you can fathom now why the traditional way of saving our money in the savings account won't benefit much. In the long run, inflation will hamper our returns and the money will remain stagnant (in its value) or even decrease. But yes, savings accounts are the safest option (with null risk). If you want to grow your money by taking a bit of risk then follow on.

5.2 Fixed Deposit

Financial Institutions feature special savings options that are better than the traditional savings account. **Fixed Deposits** and **Recurring Deposits** are the two most favored investment options in India. While these are somehow better than a savings account, you have fewer chances that your money will grow. Indian banks offer an average of 5-7% interest rates on FD/RD.

In a Fixed Deposit scheme, you pay a certain sum of money (one time) and the bank pays an interest on it. You get that money at the end of the maturity period (with the interest accumulated). While in Recurring Deposit, your bank debits a fixed amount from your account every month.

The rate of interest varies from bank to bank. FD is a good option for the ones who have accumulated a sum of money and want to invest in a better option than keeping it in the savings account. The RD option is for those who want to make saving a habit and desire to contribute part of their income every month.

There are also **tax-saving fixed deposits** in which you need to invest your money for a lock-in period of 5 years. You can claim tax benefits under Section 80C of the Income Tax Act. Even so, it is important to note that the returns earned here are taxable.

5.3 Stocks

It is a vast topic and needs an in-depth explanation. Many of us from the Science and Humanities background fear to come to the stock market 'game' as we have this preconception that it's risky and/or illegal. But, I will try to bust all the myths regarding the stock market in just a minute. But before that, let me address the question, What is a stock market?

Every company starting from cosmetics to mobile telecom operators, from the health industry to car businesses have an ownership system. If a small (or big) company wants to raise its business or for any other purpose wants capital, it can dilute its ownership in the form of "Shares". They come online, file an IPO (Initial Public Offering), and decide to sell x amount of shares for a set amount of price. In this way, we can purchase the shares and become an owner of the company (yes, you own the company!) but your ownership in the company might not be so high (as percentage).

For such investing in the stocks, you have to make three types of accounts:

- **Demat Account:** It is the account in which all the purchased shares are parked. Demat accounts can be created by anyone with a Broker (Example: Zerodha, Upstox, Groww, etc.) These brokers provide several services like showcasing the past performance of a company, perform purchasing and selling of stocks (or shares), etc. For this, you need to pay a charge called *brokerage*.
- **Trading Account:** It helps an individual investor to buy and sell shares. The trading account can be with the same broker or with another.

- **Bank (Savings) Account:** Last but not the least, one needs a bank account from which the money is debited/credited when the sells are bought and sold. All these accounts should be linked.

Investing in the stock market needs a lot of research; you shouldn't blindly follow someone and get your money wasted. Before diving into the core concept of investing in the Stock Market, let's bust some common myths that we hear in our daily lives.

Myths about Stock Market Investing

- It is risky and illegal: Yes the Stock market is extremely risky if you do not know the right way of investing. It is said, Risks and Returns go hand-in-hand, hoping for high returns means there would be high risks. And on the illegal statements: No, except "Insider trading", the stock market is completely legal and you can join the league of value Investing of stocks without a second thought. Just research, learn and then put money.
- It's difficult for me: Firstly, this is not a myth, it is just a self-limiting thought that you have right now. Every new thing seems difficult and unattainable from outside when we have less knowledge about it. Stock Market feels daunting at first but with time, you will gain expertise in it.
- It's late for me/It's early for me: This is a common myth. If you are in your twenties, your risk-taking capabilities are high; you have nothing to lose now (except money). You have every opportunity to learn and make mistakes and doing so you can improve your knowledge about money.

So, yes if you are young then you can take risks. Although, I won't recommend it to those people who are in their late years. Try focusing on other aspects of investment options.

- I don't have the right education: Investing in stocks doesn't need an MBA. Decent knowledge in math will suffice. Moreover, it is said getting too much information will do no good. You will suffer from Analysis Paralysis (An inability to make decisions due to over-thinking a problem).

Stock Market Terminologies

1. *Bear/Bull Market*: The chances that the market will go up or down depends on various factors and no one can predict that. But, if you are optimistic that the market will rise, then you are a Bull and the market is termed as Bull Market. Contrarily, if you think that the market will lose its value (in points) then you are a bear. The market is called a Bear Market.

2. *Dividends*: Most companies distribute a part of their profit made during the year among the shareholders. Of course, the company decides if it will share the dividends to the shareholders or invest back in their business to earn more profits. Dividends are announced by the company (Board of Directors) on the **Declaration Date**. And on a certain date called the **Ex-Dividend Date**, if you hold the shares in your Demat Account, then you are entitled to get the dividend. This Ex-dividend date is earlier than the **Record Date** (The date on which you *must* be on the company's books). Finally, you get the dividend paid to you on the **Payment Date**.

3. *Holding period:* After you buy shares, they are stored in

your Demat account which you can hold for as long as you want. This is termed the holding period. The holding period may vary from a minute to as long as forever. The Holding period depends on the type of investing you do:

- Intraday: When the stock/share is bought and sold on the *same day* and the orders are squared off before the end of the trading day. It is also known as Margin Intraday Square off (MIS).
- Delivery: If the purchased stocks are sold after the date of purchase (keeping it for at least one day), then it is referred to as Delivery or Cash N Carry (*CNC*).

4.*OHLC*: It stands for open, high, low, and close.

- *Open* is the price at which the stock opens for the day.
- *High* is the highest price at which the stock trades during the day.
- *Low* is the lowest price at which the stock trades during the day.
- *Close* is the closing price of the stock.

5. **Intrinsic Value:** It is the indicator of what the worth of a stock is. Sometimes, a stock may be undervalued (cheap) while sometimes it is overvalued (expensive). It is on us, that we buy the stock at a value that is the actual worth of the stock (Intrinsic Value). Pro-Investors look out for companies that are cheap to buy right now but have a good future.

6. **Volume**: Volume is counted as **the total number of shares that are actually traded** (bought and sold) during the trading day or specified set period. Comparing the volume of

a company at present to the past, we can get a clearer idea, if people's interest in that company is going up or down.

7. **Return on Equity** (*RoE*)*:* Roe is a measure of the financial performance of a company calculated by dividing Net Income by shareholder's equity. For investing in stock, check if the RoE is high as compared to its rivals in the same industry or sector. An ideal RoE should be 15%.

8. **Market Capitalization***:* The total value of a company in terms of its outstanding shares. It is calculated as,

Market Capitalization = Share price x Total Number of shares.

9. **SEBI***:* It goes with the full name of **Securities and Exchange Board of India**. It is the regulatory authority of the stock market. It is entrusted with the task to regulate the Indian Capital Market. It safeguards the interest of investors and aims to inculcate a safe investment environment by implementing several rules and regulations as well as by formulating investment-related guidelines.

10. **CDSL/NSDL**: CDSL(Central Depository Services Ltd.) and NSDL(National Securities Depository Ltd.) are the two bodies that maintain our Demat Account(the place where our shares are parked). These depositories act as the vault for the shares that we purchase. They also transform our physical shares into Dematerialized (Demat) format.

11. **T+1 Day**: After you buy or sell the share(s), it takes 1 day (24 hours) to reflect in your Demat account. This is called the 'T+1' settlement. So, for example, if you buy a share on a specific day (called the Trading 'T' day), the shares will get reflected in your Demat account after 1 working day. The same goes for the seller in which if he/she sells share(s), the amount gets credited after 1 working day. Earlier, it was T+2 days for settlement of shares.

12. **Alpha**: It is basically the difference between a particular stock (of choice) and the actual return provided by the market (measured through the index). It thus measures the performance of a stock or investment instrument in comparison with the benchmark i.e., Market Index. Alpha could be negative, positive, or zero (same return as of the market). Let's see an example, If a stock gives a return of 15% in a particular time frame and the market had given a return of only 10%, then we can say that the stock has an positive alpha of 5%.

13. **Beta**: Depending only on the metric of alpha for measuring a stock is vague. Another key point is Beta which determines the 'relative' risk or volatility of an investment instrument. Beta of 1 means that the volatility of a stock is roughly equal to the volatility of the overall stock market (Index). Beta greater than 1 signifies that a stock is riskier than the market, and a beta lower than 1 signifies the opposite.

In simpler terms, look for stock or any other investment option which has the '**Highest Alpha and Lowest Beta**'.

Alpha and Beta are historic metrics that are calculated by measuring the past performance. Thus it may not accurately predict the future performance.

Stock Market Investing is a game of emotions.

The two main emotions that are linked in the share market are *Fear* and *Greed*. The volatility that is seen in the stock market is greatly attributed to these two emotions.

When people are optimistic that the market will go up in

value, they act bullish and invest hugely (due to their greed). This causes a change in the market condition (Going up). On the other hand, if people are pessimistic about the market, they will act bearish and withdraw from the market or will halt their new investment plans (due to fear). This causes a change in the market condition as well (going down).

So, now it is clear why the market prices fluctuate so much. Other factors that contribute to the fluctuation are News (Positive or Negative), Demand and Supply, etc. Our success in the stock market is greatly influenced by this factor: *How well do we control our emotions?*

What is the right time to buy or sell a stock?

Honestly, there is no direct answer to this. Warren Buffet says, "Be fearful when others are greedy and be greedy when others are fearful." This can also be paraphrased as: Buy when others are selling, sell when others are buying. The market emotion a.k.a Market Mood is quite difficult to contemplate, but there are some tools you can find online to get hang of the condition of the market.

Go to this site called: https://bit.ly/3yKtVRb. Here you will find what the mood of the market is right now.

Before deciding to buy a stock, ponder why in the first place you want to buy that stock? Were you allured by the business model of the company? Did anyone suggest it to you? Or Is it just that you need to pick a stock and so any stock will do?

Whatever the case is, you need to keep in mind that the stock market is a long-term investment. You can't blindly throw a knife and choose the best stock out there, without doing any research.

You are investing your hard-earned money so go for companies that have a chance to grow in the future and can multiply your money. In this perspective, new companies have a vast scope of growth but that comes with the *risk* of failure too. Big and old companies are less risky (stable) but have little chance of showing exponential growth.

Selecting (Buying) a decent stock:

- Be an Investor, think for the long term, and invest in companies that will survive for a long period.
- Check on Return on Equity.
- See if the profits are escalating gradually each year.
- Go through the Balance Sheet of the company and check if there are excess debts and liabilities. Avoid companies with high debt levels.
- Check if there are any cases against the management.

Now that being said, you are aware of how to buy a stock. But, now when to sell a stock?

Selling a stock:

- Sell a stock as soon as your goal is fulfilled.
- Consider selling if there is a change in the management and you have doubts about the new management.
- You might consider selling if the debt level is increasing; the profit is negligible or stagnant.

With time, the experience in investing in the stock market will increase manifold.

5.4 Mutual Funds

Overwhelmed with the idea of researching and then choosing the right stock? If you don't want to work hard but want to achieve decent returns, better than the savings account, Mutual Funds come in handy. Mutual Fund is a burning topic these days. Be it TV ads, friends and family, everyone pushes you to buy or invest in Mutual Funds. But why this hype?

Mutual Funds are nothing but a basket of stocks put together, managed by an **Asset Management Company** (AMC). It is just stock market investing but now it is done by someone other than you. AMCs collect all the money from us (Investors) and choose which stocks to pick according to their intuition. They can be right or wrong as the market is highly unpredictable and volatile.

Even so, it is a safer option as in a mutual fund; there are various stocks inside it. So, if one company fails to perform well and its stock price decreases, other stocks can cope up. But, there is a catch. Mutual funds companies will charge you a fee for their service and that might reduce your returns.

For selecting a profitable mutual fund, look for the following criteria:

- **Expense Ratio**: In Investing, fees are your enemy. One such fee is the Expense Ratio, the charge you need to pay the mutual fund companies for helping grow your money. Some mutual funds charge low, while some high. Look for the expense ratio of potential funds and then choose the one with the lowest. The ideal expense ratio should be somewhat between 0.5% to 0.75%. An expense ratio of more than 1% seems to be okay for some, but remember in the long run, it will crush your returns dramatically.

- **Exit Load:** There are some charges that you need to pay for exiting a mutual fund (early than the set period). This is called the Exit load. Choose a mutual fund that has a lower exit load, because you don't want to compromise with your returns. An ideal exit load should be less than 1%.
- **Risk Profile:** Depending on your risk appetite, choose the one which has a lower risk than the one which is high in risk. This of course depends directly on your 'Goals'. For example, if you want to buy a house about 10-15 years from now, you can take a calculated risk and invest in long-term mutual funds (or Equity funds) as they have a greater chance that your money will increase in value. Whereas, if you want to save money for your marriage (4-5 years from now), then invest in Debt funds that are less risky and give you decent returns.
- **Check the past performance*:** Even if the past performance of mutual funds(also stocks) does not ever indicate the future performance, it only shows how well the asset manager of that mutual fund has performed in the past. Check the history of a mutual fund for at least 5 years or more, and then compare it with its peers. If the mutual fund performed better than its peers that means the asset manager did a commendable job. You can probably think of investing your money here.
- **Assets under Management (AUM):** AUM is not a clear indicator but only gives a subtle idea of the size and success of a given fund house. A high AUM means you get higher liquidity and can take out your money when required.

Types of Mutual funds:

- Based on **Sectors** (IT, Pharmaceutical, Energy, etc.)
- Based on **Market Capitalization** (Large Cap, Small Cap, Multi-Cap, etc.)
- Based on **Taxes** (Tax-saving funds and Non-Tax-saving funds) and others.
- Based on **Risk Factor** (Equity Funds and Debt Funds).

Index Funds

Before discussing Index Funds, let us first comprehend what Index is. India has two main **Stock exchanges** namely National Stock Exchange (NSE) and Bombay Stock Exchange (BSE). All the companies that want their shares to be traded need to register themselves under NSE and BSE.

To measure the performance of the market as a whole, there is something called an Index which acts as the barometer of the market. These Indices are Nifty 50(NSE) and Sensex (BSE). In Nifty50, there are present-day top 50 Stocks (Companies) ranked by their Market Capitalization and in Sensex, the top 30 companies are put together.

In short, Indices are a dynamic basket of top companies and are an indicator of the consuming capacity of the consumers or the state of the economy as a whole.

So, now what do we mean by Index funds? These are nothing but funds or investment instruments that invest the money in these Indices. Since we invest directly in these Indices, there is minimal cost of management and no hefty charges of research. When we look for long-term investment, Index funds are a safer option as we don't need to be fearful of the daily volatility of the market because, in the long run, the stock market will go higher.

Equity-linked Savings Scheme (ELSS)

These are special types of Mutual funds and are tax-saving investment options. ELSS has a lock-in period of 3 years and there is no premature exit. In ELSS, you can avail tax exemption of up to Rs 1.5 lakh (Under 80C). The ELSS fund invests the money in Equity and Equity-linked instruments (a minimum of 80%). You can start investing in ELSS with a minimum contribution of Rs 500.

How to invest in mutual funds?

There are two methods by which you can invest in the market. The mutual fund companies will give you either an option to invest a minimum amount every month for a set period. This systematic investment in Mutual Fund done every month is called SIP (Systematic Investment Plan). The other method is by investing a 'one-time amount' called Lumpsum investment. Both have their pros and cons.

```
Tip: While investing in the stock or mutual funds,
keep in mind that the past performance of any
company/fund will not guarantee future performance.
```

Understanding RETURNS

Returns are usually expressed in terms of annual yield. There are two methods to calculate our return.

1. **Absolute Returns:** This is the return that we generate from our investments (or trades) and is absolute. Here the period is not taken into consideration.
2. **Compounded Annual Growth Rate (CAGR):** It is a representational number/rate that can be utilized to calculate the return of almost any investment instrument. It is one of the most accurate ways to find the returns for anything, assuming the profits were reinvested at the end of each year. CAGR can also be used to compare two or more investment options, although it does not give the idea of the risk involved. The CAGR uses a similar formula as of the compound interest.

5.5 Gold and other metals

Gold has been one of the best investment options in the past decade. The investment term related to gold and other precious metals is called *Bullion Investing.*

Investing in metals is less risky and also allows diversification. Investing in Commodities like gold is thought to be a safer option. In the past too, whenever there was a downfall or crash in the market, people went for safer, less risky options to safeguard their portfolio against huge losses. Even though it has some major downsides:

- Fear of Loss and theft.
- Making Charges.
- Taxes on selling and purchasing.
- High volatility in its price.

But of course, there is a solution to that. If you want to invest, you can purchase digital gold (online) or else the Sovereign Gold Bonds (SGB) issued by the Government.

Sovereign Gold Bonds

It is simply the best way of investing in Gold. SGBs are a form of government securities that are issued by the Central Bank of India, RBI on behalf of the Government of India. SGBs are substitutes for holding physical gold. Investors have to pay the issue price in cash and the bonds will be redeemed in cash on maturity. These days, SGBs can also be bought online. An individual can buy anywhere between 1 gm and 4 kg in any given fiscal year.

One gains a 2.5% interest on the initial value of the purchased gold. This interest is taxable as per your tax slab. But there is no capital gains tax when redeemed at the maturity period which is 8 years. Hence, the liquidity here is very low. SGBs are safe in the perspective that these are backed by the government of India itself. There is some risk involved in SGBs i.e. risk of capital loss if the market price of gold declines. However, the investor does not lose in terms of the units of gold that he has paid for.

Though the tenure of the bond is 8 years, early encashment/r edemption of the bond is allowed only after the fifth year from the date of issue. The bond will be tradable on xchanges if held in Demat form. It can also be transferred to any other eligible investor.

5.6 Real Estate

It can be full-time or part-time investing. Investing in Real Estates and Property is quite tedious as it needs much paperwork, a corpus of money, and research. In real estate, one invests in the physical property like land, buildings, etc. It has further sub-niches. You can decide your forte in which you are interested.

The success in real estate depends mainly on the area (Demographics) and the economy (purchasing power of the people).

In the past, many people have been conned due to various reasons. But, in recent times, there are stringent rules especially made to protect the consumers from being exploited. The margin rate (the difference in the purchase price and the selling price of an asset) which was awful 20-30 % in the past has come down to 8-10% in today's market.

Investing in Real Estate needs proper knowledge, time, and patience. You can't become a millionaire overnight. But it has huge prospects if done well.

5.7 Other Investment Options

This includes investments like Cryptocurrency, Forex Trading (Investing in Foreign Exchange), Bonds, Non-Fungible Tokens (NFTs), etc.

Cryptocurrency

It is a sweet-sour investment option. It is risky and highly volatile. In the past, Bitcoin, one of the highly proclaimed investments in cryptocurrency, has given a huge return. It is due to the following facts:

(a) There are only a limited number of bitcoins available to be mined. (Precisely 21 million or 2.1 Crores)

(b) It is a decentralized system i.e., not a single entity owns or has control over it.

(c) It is a safer option to transact in Bitcoin as it is backed up by a trustless public ledger. There are specific individuals called "Miners" who verify the transactions done in Bitcoin. Irrespective of the value that a bitcoin stores now, it has some downsides too. It is volatile, use of Bitcoin for illegal works; transactions once done can't be reverted.

NFTs

These are special tokens of any class (music, image, video, etc.) which are stored in a unique cryptographic way that is difficult to replicate. Hence the uniqueness makes it a valuable product and invest-worthy. Anyone with appropriate knowledge can make NFTs and sell it to others.

Bonds

These are relatively unpopular investment options for an average Indian. Bonds are financial instruments included in the debt asset type (Non-equity). These are issued by governments or private organizations to raise funds from the general public. One of the most heard bond we discussed earlier and that was SGBs. Other bonds include Government Bonds (also called Government Securities or G-Secs), Corporate Bonds, Municipal Bonds and so on. There are also certain specific types of bonds with a special purpose like Masala Bonds (rupee-denominated bonds for raising capital from outside India), Green Bonds (raised for environmental projects), Blue Bonds (raised for marine and ocean projects), etc.

We are now quite aware of the popular Investment Instruments in India.

Rule of 72

In every investment that you do, you can find how long (in years) it will take to double your money. Just get the rate of interest. Divide 72 by the rate. The output will tell you the time in which your money will double.

$$T = 72/r$$

6

Asset Allocation

"Risk comes from not knowing what you're doing."
- Warren Buffet.

The allocation of Assets is probably the most important step in money management. Furthermore, Asset Allocation is also a must because it enables you to build a portfolio based on the principle of **Diversification**.

You might have heard this saying, "Never put all your eggs in one basket". That is what diversification does. It is the idea of dividing our assets, investment, etc. in various instruments such that your loss is minimized. Diversification prevents you from becoming broke because the chances that *all* of your investments will fail at one time is negligible.

Let's come to the asset allocation part again. Asset Allocation is performed, based on your risk profile (How much risk one can take in accordance to his/her age, income, dependents, etc.) and growth requirements (How much do you want your money to grow?) For example, young investors who are in their 20s can take higher risks than those who are in their late 60s or 70s.

A budding investor will learn a lot in his initial stages so taking risks is justified. S/he has got no dependents to look after and has a whole life ahead. Moreover, the only thing in life you regret are not the risks that you take but the risks that you don't take.

So, following your risk appetite, you can build a **Balanced Portfolio**. An ideal portfolio should have a combination of stocks, gold investments, bonds, mutual funds, etc. This gives the portfolio a safety net of *Diversification*.

To get an idea about how to manage the process of asset allocation, let's first understand the major types of Asset classes in India. These are:

- **Equity:** It comprises Stocks, Mutual Funds, Index Funds, etc.
- **Fixed Income:** It comprises PPFs, Fixed deposits, Recurring deposits, bonds, etc.
- **Cash:** It comprises all your cash deposits and this class is high in liquidity.
- **Real Estate and Property:** It is low in liquidity as it involves paperwork, finding the right buyer/seller, negotiating a better deal, etc.
- **Commodities:** It includes Gold, silver, copper, etc.

So, these are the major asset classes you can invest in. Now accordingly you can decide which investment options get what percentage of your portfolio based on risk profile, your age, and your requirements (to create wealth or to conserve wealth).

With the asset allocation understood, one can even find his/her Net Worth. It is simply the value of any entity, in this case the person's.

Net Worth

You must have heard that Mr. X has so and so worth. It simply means the actual value of an individual in terms of the assets that one holds minus all the liabilities that s/he owes. In order to calculate your Net Worth, first find the value of the assets that you own then deduct the liabilities from it.

Tip: As a rule of thumb, you can deduct your age from 100, the result will give you the percentage that you should think to invest in Equity funds (Stocks) and the rest goes to Debt funds. For example, if you are 24, then you should invest 76% (100-24) of your investment amount in Equity and the rest can be invested in Debt Funds (24%).

7

Tax Management

"The hardest thing to understand in the world is the income tax."
- Albert Einstein.

Undoubtedly, this chapter would be one of the few chapters in this entire book that you can't miss. It is yet another important aspect of money management. Taxes are a crucial part of the economy of any country. The taxes that we pay are used by the government to run its welfare schemes, pay pensions to people in older age groups, and perform various other operations. The government acquires a major portion of its income through taxes that we all pay in the form of Direct and Indirect taxes. Without taxes, the government can't run the economy and the country as a whole.

The money that we earn from any source (investments, businesses, jobs, etc.) is our **Income**. And the tax that we pay on this Income is called the Income Tax. To reduce your Income Tax liability, we need to follow some Tax-saving options which are briefed at a later portion of the chapter.

Before that, let's break the concept of the Tax System in India.

7.1 Taxation System in India

India needs help from all of the countrymen in developing a tax culture. The Fear of the income tax department can only be removed by gaining knowledge of basic rules and regulations.

In India, we have a Taxation system that can be broadly categorized into two:

- Direct Taxes: The tax which is levied on an individual and *cannot* be transferred to another is called the Direct Tax. S/he is supposed to pay the liable taxes directly to the tax authorities in India. Example: Income Tax, Capital Gains Tax, Corporate Tax, etc.
- Indirect Taxes: The tax which is levied on one individual and *can* be transferred to another is called the Indirect Tax. Here, someone other than the individual pays the tax on his/her behalf. Example: Goods and Service Tax and Value-added Tax etc.

Note: In the context of money management, we shall get familiar with the Direct Tax for Individuals and the nitty-gritty of Tax Saving.

Income Tax

It is a tax levied by the government of India on the income of every person. The provisions of the Income Tax law are provided in the Income-Tax Act (1961).

Income tax is to be paid by individuals following the position that they occupy in the tax slabs. These tax slabs are set by the government. In short, income tax needs to be filed based on the income that one earns every financial year.

Government categorizes our income as follows:

❖Income from **Salary.**

❖Income from **Business and Profession.**

❖Income from **House Property.**

❖Income From **Capital Gain.**

❖Income from **other sources** (such as dividends, interest from fixed deposits, royalty income, winning on lottery, etc.

Capital Gains Tax

Capital Gains taxes are the taxes that are levied when you gain a profit by the sale of 'Capital Asset'. Let me provide you with an example. Let's suppose your father has gifted you a property which you keep for a few years and later at some point in time, you decide to sell it off. Now, the profit that you acquired after selling that property is your Capital Gain. Since this gain comes under the category 'Income', you need to pay a tax on this (Capital Gains Tax).

Capital Gains can be of various types. We shall discuss the ones that are linked to the "Market". These are of two types:

(i) **Short Term Capital Gain(STCG):** If you liquidate your assets (Stocks or Mutual funds) before 1 year (365 days) of purchase, then it will be termed as Short term capital gain (or loss). It will directly attract a tax of 20% (as on July, 2024).

(ii) **Long Term Capital Gain (LTCG):** If you liquidate your assets (Stocks or Mutual funds) after 1 year (365 days) of purchase, then it will be termed as Long term capital gain (or loss). If the gain is over 1 lakh, It will attract a tax of 12.5% (without indexation).

7.2 Income Tax Filing

Income tax filing is the process of paying your taxes online or offline. It can be done by using Income Tax Return (ITR) Forms. Information filed in ITR should pertain to a particular financial year. It contains information about the person's income and the taxes to be paid on it during the year.

Financial Year (FY) is the year that marks the actual year the income was earned. In India, the Financial Year starts from 1st April and ends on 31st March (the next year). And the income tax is paid in the next year (called the Assessment Year). So, if FY is 2019/20, the AY would be 2020/21.

The major ITR forms in India have been illuminated as follows:

ITR 1- It is most commonly known as Sahaj Form. ITR1 needs to be filed by resident individuals having total income *up to ₹ 50 lakhs from the following source*s:

- Salary
- One house property
- Other sources include investments, schemes or fixed deposits, etc. (Excluding winning from lotteries and income from horse races).
- Agricultural income up to ₹ 5,000.
- Individuals who do not own any assets or property in countries apart from India

ITR 2- This form is applicable for the following persons:

- People who earn income through salary or means such as a pension.
- A person whose source of income is through the sale of assets or property in India i.e. capital gains.
- Income from more than one housing property.
- People who don't earn money from any business venture.
- A person who owns assets in countries outside of India and/or earns income from countries outside of India.
- A person whose income from agriculture is above Rs 5,000.
- A person who gets his income from lotteries or horse racing.

ITR 3- This one is useful for an individual taxpayer or a Hindu Undivided Family(HUF), who solely operates as a partner in a firm but does not conduct any business under the firm. This is also applicable for individuals who do not earn any income from the business conducted by the firm.

This form is usually filed by those taxpayers whose taxable income 'earned from the businesses is only in the form of *Salary, Commission, Bonus, Interest, and Remuneration*.

ITR 4- It is for those individuals who conduct a business or who earn income through a *profession*. This form is applicable for all types of businesses, undertakings, or professions, without any limit on the income earned.

Taxpayers can also club any income they receive from windfalls, speculation, salaries, lotteries, housing properties, etc., along with the income earned from their business. An individual with any profession, right from shopkeepers, doctors, or designers to agents, retailers, and contractors, is eligible to file their ITR using this form.

Note: The other ITRs (ITR 5, ITR 6, ITR 7) are applicable only for companies and firms.

In India, if you are earning, you fall under one of the tax brackets that has been provided (as per your income) in the table:

Tax Slab for FY 2024-25	Tax Rate
Upto ₹ 3 lakh	Nil
₹ 3 lakh – ₹ 7 lakh	5%
₹ 7 lakh – ₹ 10 lakh	10%
₹ 10 lakh – ₹ 12 lakh	15%
₹ 12 lakh – ₹ 15 lakh	20%
More than ₹ 15 lakh	30%

7.3 Tax Management

We have got through the ITRs (one at a time) in the previous section. Now, comes the interesting part: *How to manage or save taxes?* This can be done in two ways: one is legal and the other is illegal.

When someone thinks of Tax filing, they think that they can hide their money from the Income Tax (IT) department and reduce their Income, and get saved from paying any taxes.

Do remember that, this way of hiding, understating, or falsely reporting your Annual Income, also called **Tax Evasion** is a crime and you are considered to be involved in a Tax Fraud. Tax evasion is illegal in India and is dealt with severe penalties and punishment.

However, there are some legal and smart ways in which you can reduce your taxable income and save taxes. Here, we shall cover those valuable tax management tips that every taxpayer should make use of.

Under the new tax slab, the income tax rates has been reduced and so, you are not given the option to take the benefits of Exemptions and Deductions. But if you opt to pay your taxes with the old tax slab, then the coming section is going to be fruitful.

Ways to save tax

Step 1: Calculate your **Gross Total Income** for the Year. Be honest, include everything. Yes, even that Diwali bonus and the winning from the lottery. You should not try to hide your income.

Step 2: Next, take all the **Exemptions** that you can opt for. Exemptions/ Allowances are part of the Gross Income that is exempted from being calculated as your taxable income. Exemptions are a legal way to reduce the amount of income that is subject to income tax. Several provisions could be used to reduce your Gross Total Income by the use of Exemptions. Income Tax Exemptions are covered under *Section 10, 11, 12, 13, and 24* of the Income Tax Act.

A few examples of income tax exemptions include house

rent allowance (HRA), leave travel allowance (LTA), children's education allowance, etc. After the exemption is deducted from the Gross Total Income, it is referred to as the **Taxable Income**.

Step 3: Further reduce your Tax liability by proper use of **Deductions**. Income Tax Deductions are investments made during a financial year that offset (or deduct) against the taxable income. After the deductions are used, the remaining portion of the income is the Net Taxable Income. Income tax deductions are mostly covered under Section 80 of the Income Tax Act.

Let's go through few sections and their benefits:

- Under **Section 80C,** you can take a maximum deduction of Rs 1.5 lakh. This deduction includes investments in PPF, Children's Tuition fees, ELSS, National Savings Certificate(NSC), Principal Repayment of home loan, among others.
- Under **Section 80D**, you can take deductions for health insurance premiums and medical expenses for senior citizens. Individuals below 60 years can claim up to ₹25,000; whereas senior citizens can claim up to ₹50,000.
- Under **Section 80TTA**, Income of up to ₹10,000 earned from interest on savings accounts can be claimed.
- Under **Section 80E**, you can claim deductions on Interest paid on an education loan.

You can check other sections too. Some of the most popular tax deductions are investments made in the Equity-linked savings scheme (ELSS), Public Provident Fund (PPF), National Pension Scheme (NPS).

With this, we come to the end of tax planning.

Tip: You have the option to choose between the old tax regime (with exemptions and deductions) or the new tax regime (without exemptions and deductions) while filing your ITR.

8

The Power of Compounding

"The greatest invention of Mankind is the Compound Interest."

- Albert Einstein.

Money has a huge potential in the sense that money can make money. And it is proved by the concept of Compounding, the eighth wonder of the world. When you see the life of Warren Buffett and zoom in on the intricacies of his wealth made over the years. You will find that he started investing at the age of 10 years but the fruit ripened only after the age of 30 (when his net worth was $1 Million) and then it boomed again after he attained 52 years.

This could be a great example to help you get the idea of how money can double, quadruple, and so on. The only thing that matters is that you *invest in instruments that can fight inflation and that you invest early.*

Throughout this journey, you have been illuminated with all the famous instruments that you can invest in. Now it's your turn to act. If you work diligently and follow all the principles as stated in this book, you can just sit back and relax. Let compounding take its effect.

Remember that money grows slowly and short-term growth won't surprise you. The fruit will be the sweetest when you wait. The secret of attainment of "Good Money" is Compounding. It is the simplest formula.

Let me give a clearer idea about how compound interest works and how it varies from 'simple interest'. In simple interest, the interest is given only on money that is put, called the principal while in the compound interest, the interest is given on the principle as well as the interest accrued from the last year, and the process continues. So, we can fathom the idea that compound interest helps our money to grow manifold.

Let's go through a simple example. Suppose we have put 10,000 Rs and the rate of interest is 10 % PA.

Principal	10,000 Rs	10,000 Rs
Time (in years)	Simple Interest	Compound Interest
1	1000	1000
2	1000	1100
3	1000	1210
4	1000	1331
5	1000	1464.10
Total Interest Earned	5000	6105.10

This is just for 5 years, you will be amazed how much your money will grow if you keep it for 20, 30, 40 years, or more.

The compounding effect that we have just seen depends on various factors:

1. **Time period:** Time is the most crucial factor in wealth creation. A few years' delay in investing will reduce the corpus drastically. So, starting early is the best decision. Compounding doesn't rely on earning big returns. Merely good returns sustained for the longest period possible (especially in times of chaos) will always win.

2. **Rate of Interest:** The schemes that have been discussed throughout the book have differences in their Interest rate. Choose the ones with higher rates.
3. **Tax:** Tax chunks out a major portion of your income and investment. Before devoting yourself to investing in various schemes, find how much you need to pay as taxes for the gains that you make. Also, get a clear idea about how to reduce your taxes by legal means.
4. **Compounding frequency:** It is also a decisive factor. The quarterly compounding frequency will have a higher interest rate than the monthly and yearly.

Do it Yourself: To experience the power of compounding, visit this site https://bit.ly/3duz5sF.

- Enter any suitable amount that would be considered as a principal amount (Let's take it 1,00,000 Rs).
- Enter the Interest rate (Let's suppose 10%).
- Enter the period (Let's suppose you started investing at 30 and will retire at 60, the time the money will grow in between these will be 30 years)
- Let the Compounding frequency be yearly.
- The total corpus you will have gained will be "₹**17,44,940**".

This is the supreme power of compounding. The more time you give your investments, the more it can grow.

9

Self-Investment

"An Investment in knowledge pays the best interest."
- Benjamin Franklin

Through the book, We learned money management techniques, ways to increase our income, wealth creation, saving for retirement, etc. Another important point that I want to add is to Invest in our own lives.

We can have millions in our bank account, we might spend a lot to help someone. But, if you don't use that money to grow, it won't benefit you in the long run. Investing in ourselves will skyrocket our productivity in numerous ways. With increased productivity, we can work more efficiently, and thus our value in society will increase.

You can invest in yourself in myriad ways. Some of them include:

1. **Making healthy lifestyle choices**: Maintain a balance between your work (Profession) and your personal life,

keeping your health as your top priority. Health is our greatest asset. So, don't ever compromise with that. Good health will allow you to enjoy wealth.

2. **Never stop learning**: You may be a master in your profession, even so, try to gain expertise or at least survival skills in other fields as well. Attend seminars (or webinars) on the topic that intrigues you. Have a discussion on the ideas and philosophies with an accomplished individual. This will broaden your thinking and you might gain valuable wisdom. You have to acquire new skills to cope with the competition out there.

3. **Reading good books**: As already proclaimed by many: Leaders are Readers. You don't have the time to do all the things, make mistakes, and then learn from them. The best way to gain knowledge is to read books written by great minds. It saves the time and energy that would have been wasted if you had to gain the knowledge on your own. There are ample books that can provide you with a clearer idea of any topic. There is a quote that says, *"A person who won't read has no advantage over one who can't read"*.

4. **Travel**: Fresh ideas won't strike your mind if you stay in one place forever. You need to go out and discover your truths and values for life. Travel also encompasses a vibrant point of view, rejuvenates your mind, and cleanses your soul. So, take out your passport and have this enriching experience in your life.

5. **Managing Time**: Time is the second most important asset. Spend good quality time doing things that you value the most. The time that you give to your family and friends can't be bought with money. Thus, managing time is

indispensable and thus will help you grow in life. Never waste a single minute of your life, doing things that don't add value to your life.

6. **Be grateful and enjoy life**: We are so focused in our lives complaining about things that we don't have, that we lose sight of the things that we do have. So, stop complaining, be grateful for whatever you have. Ponder upon sharing whatever you can. Volunteer for any good cause. In short, *Enjoy* life.

7. **Networking**: During your early years, grow your social circle. Connect with people from different fields. Share your ideas with others, listen to theirs too. This will open up your thinking spectrum and broaden your horizon. Also, making new friends might deepen your view about others and this will upgrade your communication and emotional skills.

8. **Sleep:** Sleep is the utmost thing for a healthy body and mind. An adult should get an average sleep of 7-8 hours a day. Proper sleep is essential as the brain performs most of the cleaning process by removing the toxins, builds and strengthens neural networks, etc. It also increases our productivity.

This was just some of the ideas of how you can invest in yourself. Next, we have the last chapter of this book.

10

The Power of Giving

"We make a living by what we get, but we make a life by what we give."
- Winston Churchill

Money is good for three major things: FUN, INVEST, and GIVE. You did use the money for the first two. Now you have to give back what you have earned. The third point is **Give**.

Money can buy you almost anything but Happiness and Satisfaction. Money occupies a small portion of our life. We need good relationships, acceptance, trust, respect, and many other things that are acquired by our attitudes.

There will be a time in our life when we just have to stop. We all need a goal, and when we successfully reach that goal, it's time to halt. It is crucial to decide that final goal, which will be your *Enough*.

In the beginning, I have urged you to decide on a set amount that you feel you need for your financial freedom. If you have still not found that, ponder upon it honestly. How much do you truly need for a decent life, for your retirement, etc? Now, scribble it down in your journal or any other place. This will act as your Goalpost.

After you have achieved that, get the rest of the money donated for a good objective.

- Give your valuable time for a better world. You will feel so ecstatic, full of satisfaction.
- Teach small children and in return, you will learn from them too.
- Leave a legacy behind for the next generation.
- Be of some value to the society. Create a change (however small it may be).
- Share your wisdom, and your experiences gained so far.
- Learn from great philosophical and philanthropic minds.

Acknowledgement

This is a special portion of the book for the author. Who to thank first? Many have enthusiastically put their efforts into this work. I am deeply obliged and humbled to get such supporting people who made this possible. My Mom, who subtly viewed my work and gave me new ideas every time I felt brain fog. My dad supported me in the journey of attaining knowledge in the financial field. He is always curious to learn something new.

I am from a science background. I did my graduation in Botany. But even so, I felt no hurdles to get myself motivated to learn and at the same time, teach my friends and acquaintances what I am learning. Learning is a never-ending journey for me. You can always learn something (from anyone) and that age is not a barrier to it. Learning made my growth curve attain inexplicable heights. I encourage each of my readers never to stop learning. I have set my journey on a road that was untraveled by people related to my field.

I thank the editor for this book, *Priyanka Mech* who had diligently worked for proofreading and checking for consistency, moving along with me through thick and thin. There are others who have backed me up too. Thanks to all of them.

I thank you as well for choosing this book over others. More than 100 readers bought the first edition and I hope they were enlightened with some financial wisdom. This has been a wonderful experience to share with you.

Notes

Further Reads

- The Total Money Makeover (Dave Ramsey)
- The Psychology of Money (Morgan Housel)
- I will teach you to be rich (Ramit Sethi)
- Money master the game (Tony Robbins)
- Rich Dad, Poor Dad (Robert Kiyosaki)
- The Richest Man in Babylon (George S. Clason)
- The 4-hour workweek (Tim Ferris)
- One up on wall street (Peter Lynch)
- The Millionaire Next Door (Thomas J. Stanley/William D. Danko)
- Unshakeable (Tony Robbins)

* * *